Prescriptions
from the **Dock**

written and illustrated by
Douglas Wood

 A Wind In The Pines book

Adventure Publications, Inc
Cambridge, Minnesota

Dedicated...

To those who know the world always looks better from a dock.

Illustrations by Douglas Wood
Book design by Jonathan Norberg

Published by Adventure Publications, Inc.
820 Cleveland St. S
Cambridge, MN 55008
1-800-678-7006
Printed in China

ISBN-13: 978-1-59193-129-4
ISBN-10: 1-59193-129-0

Dear Reader:

Prescriptions from the Dock is based upon the medically unsubstantiated but self-evident premise that one of the finest psychotherapists in the world is an old dock. The dock should be made of wood, preferably with several loose or missing boards and a geriatric boat or two tied up to it. These conditions convey upon the dock character and credibility. Said dock should also be oriented to observe and welcome sunrises and/or sunsets, lake breezes, the occasional passing loon or mallard, and be habituated by various persons with cane poles - youngsters, mid-sters, and oldsters - in completely unpredictable and random order.

If most or all of these conditions pertain, then the stage is set for effective Therapy and for any number of valuable Life Lessons. Here are just a few - you will surely add many of your own.

P.S. If some of these scenes look a bit dated, it's only because they are. Many are based on family photos from albums that date as far back as 1935.

Take two fish and call again
in the morning.
(Dr.'s orders)

Remember...anyone who matches wits with a fish and loses, had it coming.

Never lie.
Unless the truth is
inadequate for the situation.
(Fisherman's Code)

Behold The Fisherman

he riseth up Early in the Morning
And Disturbeth the whole household

Mighty Are his Preparations

he goeth forth full of hope, and when the
Day is Far Spent he returneth,
Smelling of Strong Drink and the
Truth is not in him.

Wear pants you can wipe
your hands on.

Be nice to dogs and small kids.
They remember.

Eat jelly sandwiches.

Keep beer in a cooler.
Keep worms in a cooler.
Don't drink worms.

14

Wear a good hat,
preferably ugly.

Oil the oarlocks.

Row your own boat.

Learn small engine repair.

Read the skies.

Don't always wear sunscreen.

Listen to loons.

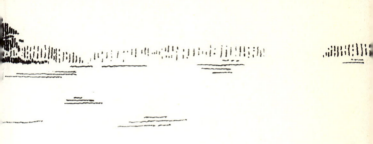

Have a favorite lure.

Sit still.

Whistle.
If you can't whistle, practice.

Carpy Diem.
Seize the fish!

Make things with your hands.

Fix stuff.
If it ain't broke,
fix it more carefully.

Fish with people much older than you.

Fish with people much younger than you.

Don't keep your feet dry.

Don't step into your tackle box.

Have rules:
Anyone who brings
a phone onto the dock
gets thrown in with it.

Notice that those who
talk most catch least.
(Fisherman's Code Supplemental)

Carry your own water.

38

Look before you leap.
But leap!

Notice that you're alive.

Remember...every day
in a beautiful place
is a beautiful day.

Ponder still waters.

Smile at your own reflection.

Always watch your bobber.

Practice optimism:
Hope the fish will bite
and sometimes they will.

Believe the fish will bite
and sometimes they will.

Know the fish will bite...
and sometimes they will.

Tie strong knots.

List the many things you won't
accomplish spending time on
docks and in boats.

Burn the list.

Look at far-away things.

Daydream.

Heed what the Greeks
said 2500 years ago:

Beauty is truth
and truth is beauty.
Rooty-toot-toot
And a rooty-toot-tooty.